A DUBLIN POET

A James Joyce 24 hour inspiration

A POEM

BY

E. Ted Gladue

COMMONWEALTH BOOKS
New York City 2019

A Commonwealth Publications paperback
A DUBLIN POET
This edition published 2019
By Commonwealth Books
All rights reserved

Copyright c 2019 by E. Ted Gladue
Published in the United States by Commonwealth Books Inc., New York

Library of Congress Cataloging-in-Publication Data

ISBN: 978-1-892986-12-2 (trade)

No part of this book may be reproduced or utilized in any form or by an means, electronic or mechanical, including photocopying, recording, or by an information storage and retrieval system, with permission in writing for the publisher, except by a reviewer who may quote brief passages in a review to be printed in a newspaper, magazine, or journal.

This work is a poem and any similarities to actual persons or events is purely Coincidental.

First Commonwealth Books Trade Edition: June 2019

PUBLISHED BY COMMONWEATH BOOKS, INC.
www.commonwealthbooks@aol.com
www.commonwealthbooks.com

Manufactured in the United States of America

This book is dedicated to

All the Kelly's of County Monaghan Ireland from where my Grandmother, Mary Kelly, a poet, was born and raised before coming to Philadelphia, Giving me the gift of poetry.
&
To all the McDermott's of County Roscommon, from where my Grandfather Philip McDermott was born and raised before coming to Philadelphia, from whom I derived my Irish citizenship and passport.

INTRODUCTORY REALITY CHECK

As always, with any of my poetry, I must first thank all my Irish pals in Philadelphia and Wildwood New Jersey who brought poetry to my heart and soul in the pubs beginning at the age of twenty-two after serving four years in the military, for no teacher in grammar school nor high school, and I might add at the university, ever inspired me to even like poetry, and it would be another twenty years before I began to write poetry, an event that was a complete surprise to me at the time that first poem burst forth from my soul in San Francisco.

On that day in San Francisco I pulled out my pen to merely record what I was seeing outside the art museum in Golden Gate Park when out popped my first poem, and a few hours later at the Cliff House Inn overlooking San Francisco bay and the magnificent Golden Gate Bridge, seals jumping on the rocks far down below, merchant ships slowly steaming out toward sea bringing to mind pals who sailed out of these very waters never to return or merchant seamen pals long lost to all but memory, the lights and shadows reflecting and playing off the windows now with only reflections of beautifully dressed men and women walking into the bar as if in a scene from Plato's "The allegory of the Cave," I took out my
Pen and wrote my second poem, "Perceptions on Black Glass," thus was born my poetry.

I had no idea where it came from, but from then on it poured out of me like free verse and then years later I discovered that my Irish grandmother, Mary Kelly from County Monaghan was a poet, which explains to some extent from where her barbarian grandson received his gift to write poetry, that by 2019 has become more important to me in attempting to understand our present mad world than all my novels, books on Chinese and American policy, and journalism here-to-fore published all around the world, the latter of which I take pride with the contention that with any given international crisis or problem I would pit my journalism against any others, such as I have from the invasion of Iraq to today's dangerous times that reminds me of 1913 worlds, this not written in arrogance, but a grace gleamed from so many of my political Ph.D. professors at the Graduate Center of the City University of New

York who had escaped Hitler, Jews, who taught me not to be afraid to be wrong, and to reject ideology, in attempting to analyze the world, to find what may be the truth.

But in today's highly charged world with so many confident egotistical media personalities shouting about how right or correct their views are, I very rarely write journalism, and am somewhat remorseful about predicting (I may have been the first journalist in America) Trump being elected President as I did President Regan fourteen years before he was elected. With so much shouting and garbage mouths in the media and public domain, we poets have a responsibility to address our world with the oldest spoken art form in the world, when flutes made out of animal bones echoed in caves as poets calmed the spirits of our ancestors with words that not only soothed the fears in their minds, but the tensions in their bodies. Speaking truth to power is a responsibility of those with knowledge of our world; but speaking truth about power is the poet's responsibility in our 21st century that appears capable of destroying all life on earth, as though it were 1988 and not 2019. Poets are obliged to leave the emphasis on writing about flowers, beautiful skies, flowing streams, heartfelt pain or happiness, and many of those things that made earlier English and American poets recognized and famous; to take their pens and put on paper the nasty realities facing our world in such poetic terms that ordinary people take notice of our dangers from a different perspective, that of art, rather than politics, if for no other reason than to save our world from the total destruction that threatens us today, as threats from another era drove me to write a book on nuclear politics that sent me in 1986 to New Zealand who had just declared itself a nuclear free zone, my hoping it would be the beginning of a trend that would spread across the world preventing the nuclear war I had feared since working in military intelligence years before, with my personal outcome of writing a novel, "Semineaux New Zealand," about my experiences at the time.

 Today threats do not demand such commitment as I expressed above, for the political dialogue of the 1980s has today descended into ideological bombastic rantings with people shouting past each other with no desire for solutions unless they back their own subjective non-compromising positions, and this is not just in the United States but world-wide, as Nationalism, once studied as a relic of the past has reared its ugly tribal head, a deadly condition that led to WW I and WW II, whose powerful weapons of war today seem like weapons used by cowboys and Indians. The next time, it ain't going to end with just buildings, infrastructure, and cities destroyed, eventually to be rebuilt. This time it will be over, for all live on earth; for history has taught us that when men develop weapons, they eventually use them against real or perceived enemies. For we are animals first, and human being secondly, for to be human is like democracy, it takes love; and their ain't much love going around these days anyplace on the planet.

Poets need to step up and forward and address our human condition in this hour of darkness; yes "hour of darkness," for all one has to do is read the world news every day, where suffering is terminal, and political solutions do not appear to be able to remedy, thus: history teaching us, war is inevitable, as it was in 1913, and nearly in 1962 at a time I was teaching Modern European History at Villanova University and how to look for signs of pending war, using 1912 and 1913 as examples, when one night, I ordered my class to the sandwich shop where they had a TV; to view President Kennedy addressing the nation about the Cuban Missile Crisis, a time when people froze in horror. Then we needed smart political minds to avoid nuclear war; today we have enough smart political minds, but they are driven more by ideology than the prudence necessary to avoid war.

Poets must speak up, as in ancient Greece, to address the threatening powers in the world. Socrates, Plato, and Aristotle were not speaking and writing as would todays intellectuals and politicians; but were dealing with critical challenges for Greece to survive as a nation and a civilization. Poetry is the only means of communication that transcends all politics and barriers to communication, for poetry is art, and art is universal and everlasting; and with its most basic power as described by Allen Grossman: "Poetry is a principle of power invoked by all of us, against our vanishing."

After over a year writing this poem I came across an obit of an
English poet, Heathcote Williams, who maintained , "If poetry
Isn't revolutionary, it's nothing. Poetry is heightened language,
And language exists to effect change, not to be a tranquilizer."
Ms. Williams gave me inspiration to continue this 4 year poem.

A DUBLIN POET

A James Joyce 24 hour inspiration

I saw a small lively happy flock of blue jays flapping wings and singing
Loudly, blue and gray feathers blowing among the leaves all lit green
As one fat little bird hung upside down and looked in my direction
This early September day, as if Summer were over.

Life in the trees, life in the trees, life in the trees….again
90 degrees , 90 degrees, 90 degrees all over
In the north and in the south
All the breezes as hot as Iraqi sands.

Today's wars for America, they are everywhere
While mine began a
Long time
Ago.

The birds are confused, the world is confused
Where are we… Oh, the oneness of planet earth?
In this year 2016
So far, so far, from what we understand.

How can you, a barbarian, write a poem
She said,
That English lady
Long ago.

And true perhaps.
At 12 when other kids were writing

Their first poems
And giggling together about their creativeness.

For here-to-fore
They had been
Secret things
Shown to nobody.

Back then, I was hiding in the woods
And along the streams,
Hiding from trauma of nuns with hate filled eyes
And older bullies with big hard banging fists, and sticks, hitting.

At 14, when my smiling classmate
Had a poem published
In some school thing
For the smart kids.

I had secrets too
Down in basement darkness
Sweat and strain, with weight that hurt
And fists and knuckles pounding, ponding, left right left right.

In winter's deep snow
Out in the darkness of night running
Running, up the snow covered hills, one step at a time
Like running in desperation for his life.

Lungs damaged by asthma
Straining, burning
Lying on mounds of freshly fallen white snow
Spitting forth years of infections.

A boy's body
Recreated, as a man
Never to be violated
Again.

I walked the dreaded paths now packed with muscle
And welcomed the many bullies who thought
In historical terms,
As I laughed at their attacks, I smiled into their confused faces.

With my new fists of iron
And strength of a bull
I could not spell, yet
But I was a man.

Whose only friends had been
The bluebirds and other flying beauties
Deep in the woods
And along the streams.

But the blue jays have returned,
As confused as refugees crossing the sea
Or gays in the American south
As deadly as life in the caliphate for a transgender mate.

Or as an Italian poet of old once wrote, of " how
Vain is every hope, each breath, How false
Is every single plan, How full of ignorance is man
Against the monstrous mistress, Death."

Life in the trees, life in the trees, life in the trees...again
The children's needs
The immigrants needs
All of life's needs.

As Yeats once dreamed
"when sleepers wake and yet still dream"
Its possible, the Irish poet tells us
"that heavens" will open.

Unless you are of color in America
But, I don't see a black man's face
Without seeing, hundreds and thousands of brothers
I have known.

They taught me to dance and box
And taught me moves on the fields and on the courts
And shared fun and laughs,
As men and brothers, in this racist nation of ours

Last night the sun was disappearing into the Gulf far to the west
But over the eastern seas rose a cone of clouds, up from the dark

Blue ones hugging the sea, a cone like pink cotton candy, holding onto
Its pink till it's peak, all white and creamy, peaceful, like the heavens above.

But tonight a cop in Oklahoma shot another
Unarmed black man
Killed him dead
In the street, far from his family.

As I once wrote of Overtown in the l980s
"they kill your sons and grandson's, those policemen,
No greater pain men can feel."
Is this 2016, 1816, or 1716???

When I look into the eyes of many old white men here in Florida,
I see suspicion, condescending weakness, and arrogance
When I look into the eyes of a black man and he does not respond
I know why... for most Black and Latino men have laughter in their souls.

But there is life in the trees, life in the trees, life in the trees...
Time when northern leaves fall from grace
To the earth beneath
Soon to covered with rain, then ice and snow, in silence & death.

Birds bring us to see the visions of Plato
Where what we see before us, all that is visible
Serves us only one purpose
To guide us to what is most important, the invisible.

Can you see pain
Can you see sorrow
Can you see happiness
Can you see love?

The visible to the invisible
From what is real
To what is not seen
Like racism in America.

As in too many cities in America
Young black men fall
And are laid beneath
Then rain, then ice, then slow, in silence.

But life goes by so fast

The old often say
So fast,
So quickly.

But what a gift to be old and slow it all down
And look behind to figure out what it was all about
When it moved so fast as if a shadow
Now cleared to see more clearly, this wonderful life.

Speaking of time, they just tore down another old Hollywood
Motel, 1950s style, the quiet simple sweat inexpensive places
Next to an old bar, once called "Oceans Eleven," where young
People played, now call "Oceans Thirteen," where old sit and stare.

It's the times I suppose
But how to link, the 1950s Arthur Godfrey show
To Jose Fernandez, baseball entertainment
And speed boats.

And lets not forget the thief here in
South Florida
Both the sleezebags
And the bums

Trump is a bully who looks
Like Mussolini
And Hillary is so power hungry she
Stayed with Bill after he got head.

But the birds are in the trees
And they have returned

Its been 56 years between
JFK/Nixon debate
And silly Hillary
And bully pulpit Trumpie

How many birds did
Fly, from Maine
To Capistrano this season
And shit along the way?

Russian fighter jets and bombers
Are killing sweet young children in Syria, using smart
Penetrating bombs to kill them in basements and hospitals,
So proud the Russian Bear, to kill so many children.

Just met a Jamaican artist
Who spoke of one world consciousness
His philosophic words as music in the air
By the sea, on a warm evening.

I swam in darkness
In dangerous surging waves that warned of
160 mph winds about to hit
Old Jamaica, this October week.

The blue jays are flying inland
They sense "Mathew" comin this way
Like Sandy did then
Far away, far up north, where they nested then.

Batten down the hatches, stock up matches
And gin, and vodka, and rum
To dim the hum of winds
That will blow away your dreamy whims.

Like yesterday's nightmare
Like you can't run, you can't swim, you cannot
Hide, from the eye
Of Hurricane Mathew, with its surging tides.

Reminders of Hurricane Sandy
That was not just a dandy, but sprung
an escape that stretched from
Atlantic City to Key West to old Havana.

Now the winds are blowing
Like the hurricane of long ago
When my baby and I once cuddled and drank and
Drank...with rope, flashlights, survival gear within reach.

I have been through so many of these
I can't imagine water coming in up to my knees
But now I know one thing for sure

That things can disappear, beyond our needs.

Like the birds in the trees, everyone has needs
Like the Ethiopian, Sudanese, Syrian, Nigerian mothers
With children to feed
Now in a lifeboat in need.

Warfare began with men in shinny armor
Swords drawn right after dawn, now the men push the buttons
To kill mothers, grandmothers, daughters, granddaughters,
Men whom those in shinny armor would kill for having no honor.

While the poets write of whispering winds and starry nights
And singers sing of loveless nights
And billions suffer with no rights
Politicians only care about looking pretty under the lights.

Since when did weather forecasters and cooks we
Now call chefs become more important
That teachers, doctors, and writers
In this age of shallowness.

When poets compose in a vacuum of silence
And rappers scream and jump
And viewers numb in acceptance
With eyes addicted to TV, to TV, to TV.

The blue jays have returned
Now hiding from hurricane Mathew

The storm missed us, that is
The physical storm, but somehow the psychological
Storm planted in our subconscious
Remains, strangely….an indescribable madness

The butterflies see it
They see us
And laugh, as children
Once did, before the storm.

We used to work out and exercise
Before the storm threat
But now we drink the vodka
Rations for that nasty time.

Thinking of last summer's trip to Dublin
Perhaps the vodka stirred
Of gloom and a rash called
The Dublin crud, still on my ear

As least I have one
Unlike my hero
With the brush
Van Gogh

Hillary laughs at Trump
Trump scrawls at Hillary
And America goes on
With today's stock market reports

The blue jays are peeking out of the trees
Perhaps hungry
Like the refugees
Everywhere, it seems

And the universities thrive these days
With intellectual refugees
Who work cheap
In the Halls of Ivy

I see bored men who retired
Starring, into space with wallets bulging with money
And eyes filled with confusion and hatred
Which is par for the course for them.

Ladies used to ask their men,
Was I good in bed last night?
Now,
They make love to other women.

The blue jays are here for the winter
Confused at what they see.

A poet once wrote of the
"Waste Land," after he was bailed out of the bank
By Ezra Pound and other Paris collaborators
And morphed into Peter O'Toole

Oh, Peter O'Toole... the greatest actor the
Stage or screen has ever produced,
As free and wild as
Our blue jays.

Do you know what city in Iraq we are going to
Invade this week? Or how many Afghan troops
We trained last week? It's ironic that no body bags
Come into Dover anymore….such a clean war.

Donald is hungry for more power
And Hillary knows what it feels like
And she wants more
Especially after veronica punctured her bubble.

We used to drive to "the coast"
To indulge, in music, sex, drugs, and dropping out
Now, we stay in place
And indulge our screens, and nothingness.

I once loved a girl in Spain
Who dove into the sea
 called Cadiz, and drowned
Or should it have been called "time"?

What happens on a Monday
I once wrote in a poem called, "goodbye Monday"
And now it is so important
To say, screw it all on Monday.

Americans are shooting cops
our first line responders
Shows how stupid our culture is
Where Central American cops rob all.

The blue jays have returned an wish this

Poem to be about nature,
Peace,
And love.

I always wanted to write like T.S. Elliot
The guy I think of as Peter O'Toole
Writing about blues and Mother Mary
And take readers into dreams.

But with our world as uncertain
As 1914... when generations disappeared
From earth, and civilization crumbled like the
Ancient ruins of the Middle East

With right wing bigots
And hatred so nasty, little
Girls so sweet get buried under tons and tons
Of concrete and reinforced steel rods.

Oh, I see the butterflies flirting with me
Flying by to peak, like a long legged young
Texas lady on a Dallas street
With colors so sexy and wings spread wide.

Jimmy Buffet still singing, a pirate over 40
Just a few friends, down to rock bottom again
But still go for younger women
Lived with several for a while.

And mother, mother ocean, still hear you callin,
And it ain't the vodka, went to Dublin last July
Then to the mountains of Western Carolina in August
 retreated home to the silver sandy beaches of Hollywood.

Pushkin and Pasternack taught me to turn the pain
Into words, love lost
And seeking, seeking.. seeking...seeking .. seeking
Love, again.

Lost them all,
With an Irish mother, I never trusted their love
None of them...like a fool

Maybe why us men with Irish mother's drink so hard.

Speaking of drinking... I wish I knew where my old pal from
McSherry's bar at third ave and 76 street, old Patty who
Washed the cars at the dealer and met all my sophisticated
Ladies, was buried, so I could put a flower on his grave.

He drank the vodka,
Smoke d the unfiltered Camels
Held with thick Irish fingers
And was my late night drinking partner, back then.

When NYC was alive like July 4th
Seven days a week,
And nights.... When ladies liked men
More than each other.

Am I a pirate?
200 years too late
You bet...even Jimmy is
A pussy today... to much DeNiro..

As Brown sings,
The senoritas don't care-oo, when you got no
DeNiro... Buffet sings, I had enough money to buy Miami
But pissed it away so fast, never meant to last.

from Honduras to Panama,
in the mountains, and at the surf
from San Jose to san Pedro Sula, the ladies laughed
and played, with gringos trying to please.

And the Russians and Chinese are laughing
While Trump and Hillary via for power
To take us further down the path
With no laughs, washing upon the surf.

The streets of Dublin spoke to me last July
Of reasons other than famine
Of why they left
My grandparents, Kelly and McDermott.

Or that James Joyce wrote
Of just 24 hours
With such velocity
To make all us writers feel so wild.

And we are,
Except for those who sit in chairs
Or walk university stairs
And smile at coeds rather than whores.

Hard women, like those who walk
The streets of Atlantic City, with fingers so
Fast who not only steal wallets, but
Cars and cash in a dash.

Oh, oh... where are the blue jays???
They came before Mathew
And then disappeared
Like all good things in the tropics.

The blue jays are back
But so are the Taliban
And Shia killing Sunni
And Sunni killing Shia

With body bags coming
Back to Dover
America no longer
Even notices

Violence is back in Kashmir
And not forgiven in
Colombia
America has back-to-back-wars, all the time.

"Give peace a chance"
John sang, a long time ago
In a place
Called SoHo.

Or, was that Shiloh
Or Verdun

What's done is done
When peace has come.

Was it the Congress of Vienna?
Or Treaty of Versailles?
That made women sigh
For all the men, were dead.

Roses are red
And violets are blue
Should poetry
be dead, not read, or said?

Like the pink flamingos I once saw
When Miami was a virgin green
With sweet orange juice
And reefs in clear blue seas.

Trump has beefs with all nominees
Hillary has too many needs
And both,
Are bringing us all to our knees.

They both talk about all our needs
Like it were a jamboree
While his needs are insane
Hillary's are needs, needs, needs.

I see hope alive in strange places
With the sparkling warm confident
Young black girls working for
McDonalds and the burger king.

I see hundreds of
Future Michele Obama's
The most amazing "First Lady"
Ever.

The first mist barely visible hanging amidst tops of tall cedar
And pines on the banks of inland canal
Its tranquil waters reflecting the dimming sunlight

This mid-October, nature revealing
The sun is dropping in its Fall dance south.

Far from noises of autos and trucks racing north and south
East and west where once Indians fished and hunted
And Murph the Surf and his gang drowned and murdered
Young ladies in Whiskey Creek.

Winds churned up this hurricane season blowing through
The mangroves then down upon the canal
Blowing the mist as if a fog rising upward to tips of
Trees high up on a German mountain.

    Let's look at a story about this "Whiskey Creek", can't blame it all on Murphy, drowning those women like he did, for all he did was put those mysterious pine colored backwaters in print so everyone could know where they are. Before that, few ventured back into those tropical woods of tropical jungle, whose slow meandering streams once harbored alligators crocs and long snakes winding through low hanging tips of branches touching the surface of the molasses stream slowing moving south in an area so quiet and lonely, where only us pirates took our slender young ladies to explore each others bodies in the solitude of natures bosom.
    Yea, Murphy exposed these secret places hidden just south of the cut through which not just Port Everglades cargo ships passed but nuclear power U.S. submarines entered for crew changes and other secret rendezvous'. No wonder Murphy decided to murder the girls here, as remote as the Hope Diamond he took in the night.
    Old mysterious Whiskey Creek, now cost money to enter the state park and built up by two universities who have put these large buildings alongside the canal after cutting down all of what nature kept in trust from millions of years ago so professors could drive into their offices and sit in sterilized rooms starring into computer screens under the pretense they are biologists studying oceans and nature. Give me a break. The state of Florida, Nova University, and Florida Atlantic University destroyed the nature here, not the Indians or Murph The Surf.

When a man meets a woman he is driven by passion
When a women meet a man she driven by fascination
When a man leaves a women he is driven by fascination
When a women leaves a man she is driven by passion.

After the storms pass
and an inventory of all the damage left behind
no inventory can ever capture or understand

the turmoil that remains in our souls, our tattered spirits.

As in war we count the dead and wounded
And try and etch them in our collective memory
With special days and holidays, but what about your
Neighbors death, as if they never existed, never were.

And then there are the Russians who targeted and bomb maternity wards and then bombed
the children under the roofs of pediatric clinics
in Syria, far from "The Cherry Orchard."

The blue jays have returned but no one sees them
High in the trees by the deep blue sea
You see them honey, you and me
Among all the bees.

Deep in the bamboo trees
That once healed
From 1968 to 1883
When people laughed and fell to their knees.

People still laugh in the Keys
Mostly fat tourist pretending to be free
Why old Key West
Is now the place to leave

The ferry to Havana I once sailed
In another lifetime
When I was young
And everything was fun

Castro was in the hills
The Mafia were still making big bills
And the bare breasted dancers
Sat on my thrill.

If this doesn't seem to make sense
Just tune in
Saturday Night Live
Or watch them sell shit on sales channels.

Is this just America?
Or our civilization

In this time, in space
With musicians on Saturday night live

Who could never have made it
On a corner of South Philly
Or in the Bronx
Or even in a zoo.

But this is modern culture with fools who sing
As stupid
And easy
As idiots in the ring.

Far from Bruce Spring a ding
Who brought us songs we sing
As we spread our wings
In summer flings.

As Austin City Limits
Test our limits
Of what is cool
And what we feel are idiots.

But we can watch football
The real kind, not soccer
To see how we can kill
Brain cells, and minds.

Now give me freedom
Or give me, ?
I don't know
For most are wrapped up in me-dom.

The wheel-chair bound physicist Stephen Hawking
Claimed lately that we had only 1000 years
Left; but, what yhe hell, I want to hear from
A biologist about that, not a guy with his head in the stars.

Looking for an over-the-road vehicle
To move and see, until I realized I had and

Traveled through all North America,
So, what's left?

Cuba, here I come
Again, not since I was
A twenty-two year old explorer
Maybe.

Most interesting men I have ever met
And easy one
Merchant ship Captains
Who kept this Ship Agent mesmerized with tales of the high seas.

Most boring men I have ever known
an easy one
Male College and university professors
Whose egos are bloated in direct proportion to their lack of courage.

Most beautiful women in the world
Wow, that's a hard one
For all women
Are beautiful.

Most beautiful place in the world to live
That's easy
Just call it
Home.

When did cooks become "chefs?"
When did weather forecasters become TV stars
When did movie stars become sages, philosophers, and intellectuals,
When America became dumbed down by our access to nothingness.

Never before in human history have we had so many
Means to communicate
Yet
We communicate less and less

And sometimes
I am afraid,
We laugh
Less and less.

And worse
I hardly see
Anyone
Kissing.

It must be done in private
For
I still see
Babies.

The guy in the suit and tie
Dressed like a statesman
Who studied in London to be an eye doctor
Who brutally murdered his own women and children
With bombs and weapons of mass destruction
We call this place, Syria, he is the President.

Taught History back then, began at Villanova
Living in a two story coal heated cottage
On the old Main Line
Called, The Smith Estate.

Just my young bride and me,
So in love,
With forest and farms and old caretakers
Who had fought in WW I

Under the command of old Colonel Smith
Whose German father built the castle the Colonel lived in
Just across the garden and up through the trees
Where only millionaires gathered, to discuss
Their shares in African mines
Over Sherry and cigars.

Strangely enough, our next residence was another
Estate from America's robber barons,
this one built by the Pittsburg steel owner, Charles Swab

On the xmass eve 2016 time hung heavy
As voices, smiles, gestures, laughter, volume
Of great pals and bothers echoed in my subconscious
Visually looking as real as the stars in the sky

And the women I have loved
Quietly looking on
As if
It were not real.

But all their spirits are gone
Beyond
Never to
Return.

And then came

New Years Eve, 2017
With TV blasting Time Square celebrations
So happy, so young, such love.

And the memory
Of my English lady of unsurpassable beauty
Clinging to me, and my two daughters
On that night in Times Square, 1976.

Reminding me of my daughters call a few weeks ago,
Suggesting that I was the one who invented, Uber,
For I took them home so I could drive my old 1964
Malibu, around town, as a gypsy cab.

No one knew

We would all be
Eventually
The Midnight Cowboy.

What is all around you?
The future
Or
Just things of the past, always there.

We talk about them and smile
As if it our eyes see it set in stone
Always to be here
Until its all gone, like all our families.

Not just love ones and friends
But even the strangers
In buses and cars
Where are they? Where are they?

I still hear their voices, so distinct
Talking or laughing
Like it is now
But it was yesterday

When they were alive
And part of
Our lives, just real
Not just in spirit.

And how is one to write
The day after one of my
Children,
Nearly died.

And speaking of deaths
Just here in Hollywood Florida
Once filled with young crazy men and women
Reduced to retirement village by 2015.

One remaining warrior of old days
Howard the bartender,

Only known by his brass knuckles
And bad-ass Wildwood past.

Guardian of McGowan's fame
Faded upon time and life
Still standing, still serving drinks
At Sportsman's Club.

Until, mother time took him
To Hollywood Memorial hospital
His big strappin hard body
And witnessed his demise, death

The blue jays have been gone for a long time
Here in Hollywood
So have young people
For a long time.

With rents so high and scarce
As if in
Dublin,
Just the same.

Except Dublin has crowds of
Sexy
Ladies,
From all over the world.

Hollywood has
Old men with
Their old ladies,
After 30 years on the job.

Now filling the spaces
Once filled by young adventures
Who cared nothing
About security.

Now gone like
Vapor in the
Distant past,
Beauty displaced by wrinkles and frowns.

The snows are high up north
Many are high up north
Winter isolation mixed
With mind altering drugs.

Winter in New England
Beyond the stone walls
Of old farms and towns
No sunlight, little life.

As young poets sit
At sunset
With large peaceful orange balls
In old Key Largo.

While there is silence
From poets in old Europe
as refugees freeze in winter
and blood flows from terrorists.

Who hate,
Like the Spanish did the Moors
And the Jews
As Catholics burned them alive.

Does human nature change?
Does history repeat itself
Is violence
In violence?

So civilized Europeans were
In 1914
Well bred and confident
That all was well.

And oops
Madness
Unleashed, and cheered around the globe
Until the gases and the chemicals

Blind men
Lungs filled with poison
Some towns lost all their men
Never to return.

The beautiful young people
Gather and laugh in Williamsburg
Prep school types
All rich and smug.

Never have to worry
About getting broken bones
Or teeth knocked out
In Basic Training.

For in America
The boys go to college
And the working men
Fight the wars.

 Boko Haram in Nigeria sent a
12 year old girl into the middle of
A morning prayer group
With a bomb to kill them all, and herself.

A Buddhist holy-man tells us
That finding happiness in life
 is not sequential: you cannot say, I will
get rich then I will be happy later.

They have found the little girl's pendant
Just 14 when they shaved her head at Sobibor
Before the gas oven, little Karoline Cohn
Her pendant the same as Anne Frank's.

The pendant engraved, "Mazel tov", in
Hebrew meaning "good luck," and like
Anne's, her birthday was inscribed
July 3, 1929, 3: 7, 1929,

It was buried deep in the mud

Of Sobibor... over which the blue jays
Have flown
Year after year, year after year, year after year.

Where have all the blue jays gone?
Where have they gone?
Oh, why are they gone?
Why? Why? Why? Why? Why?

The birds left once before
In 1968,
Then came back
Many times, in mysterious ways.

But life goes on and little blue jays are born
To fly here and fly there
In our land of the free
And home of the brave.

And here we are at the inauguration of our
45th President of the United States
Of America
January 20 2016.

And the happiest and most smiling
Person in attendance, supreme court justice
Clarence Thomas, remember?
The sexual predator.

But above it all, the transition of power
A peaceful transition, for all the
World to see
Us, America at our finest.

An old frail former President Jimmy Carter
An old frail Senator Dole
Bush, Clinton, all, all, all, all
Paying respect, this special day in America.

Even Bernie
Who
Could

Have been.

It's common place and
Miraculous
Our constitutional
Soul, this day.

The little camera very deep in my mind this day
Vaguely remembers Truman, movies of Eisenhower
But serious black and white images on this day
In 1961, John F. Kennedy.

But today
Wow, never seen so many beautiful blonds
Since
The ones I once loved.

Oh no
Don't tell me
Clarence Thomas swearing in
The Vice President.

But the show does looks too white
To reflect our America today
Everything vanilla
better to have bishop Jackson than grabbing Thomas.

Prayers this day
A few too many
Maybe a moment of silence
Called meditation was missing.

And who predicted Trump
Would win?
ETG
On April 22, 2016.

Oops... a poet
With a head
In
Politics?

But is it not poetic?
To see the new President and his First Lady saying
Good-bye to the ex-President and First Lady
Kisses, smiles, & handshakes...not poetic?

Then the physical disconnect
With the ex flying from the capital
Grounds in a helicopter
Away, away, from the center of power in America.

Lets hear some music
To break the spell of politics
Let's listen to:
"Born In The USA."

Let's celebrate
For tomorrow
Is my
Birthday, January 23rd

An Aquarian
No less
The new age of
Aquarius.

After dark went to the beach in Hollywood
To prepare my soul for tomorrow
By placing my spirit on a cusp of the sea
That has meant so much to me.

Over many decades
Dreaming of far-off lands across the sea
No matter how secure here on land
The wondering spirit of the boy in the man.

Why, why, why,
I have always asked myself
Did these Hollywood night skies, stars,
Lights of planes, ships and boats bobbing on the sea

Have such a hold on me
to go, just go, to the other ends of

the earth from the Artic to Antarctica
from the Bahamas to New Zealand.

Why, why, why
I most likely went to Dublin
Last summer, to find the roots of the
Viking, in my Irish soul.

But it was here to the beach I
Came at nights, when I lost my
Only son,
For I still cry even in the sun.

And where my son told me in a dream
To come
And find the hundred pound bale of sacred herb
To save our home he died in.

And here I am again
After so many Ladies gone forever too
And all my Hollywood friends
Gone forever too.

Sitting on Hollywood beach at night
With flashing night lights
Upon the darkness
With my soul on the edge of the universe.

And behind me,
They are all gone,
All my friends
They are gone or died.

Their houses filled with strangers
Their cars missing from the drive
Their children long gone
The music has died.

Ah, such is life
The sage says

But it don't help the heart
To know that reality.

Some would say
Now,
And old man
But it ain't over till the fat lady sings.

One more minute
Till birthday ends
It's
Over.

Pour me
A vodka
And
Tonic.

But today a strange thing happened
Sittin in me truck in a parking lot beneath
The trees, trying to figure it all out, with my leg
Outside the door...a few drops of rain hit.

The sun was high and the sky was bright blue
With small fast flying white clouds
And then,
A rainbow.

Not just any rainbow
But a special rainbow
Like the one years ago
Telling me to leave New Zealand.

Wow, my birthday rainbow
All purple along the bottom rung
Blending into a long blue line
Giving way to yellow, then orange,
Topped by a streak of red.

High in the sky
A birthday sign
Of love
And peace this year.

When the world does not seem
So near
Donald's won, but the
Girls don't like it none.

And all the girls are out there
My god,
Are they increasing some
Thousands here, and thousands there.

But...what has happened
To love???
Yeah, what has happened
To love??

Forget love,
How about just human communication
Talking
On phones, in person, by email, by letter.

The latter dead
Greater ability to communicate
Than at any time in human existence
But...silence....silence...silence.

No one speaks
No one writes
No one calls
No, no, no, no, alone, alone? Alone, alone?

Sitting on the Hollywood beach after a good swim
And there, just on this western edge
Of the gulf stream
Sailed a sinister looking nuclear submarine.

The irony,
It passed a huge ocean going cruise ship
it's long black outline against the sky
 contrasted against
the huge white multi-decked cruise ship
as a testament to the confusion of modern times.

As two small Coast Guard vessels escorted the sub
As it turned to the east
Away from the pleasure boat
And out into the sea.

Carrying enough nuclear cruise missiles
To wipe out the entire
East Coast of America, and then some,
Amen, Amen, Amen.

Roses are red
Violets are blue
And with the push of a button
We could all be dead.

And this thought
Was after my swim
And meditation
By the sea.

Sunday's can be new
Begin again
So don't be blue
Take the clue.

But here in 2017
Most I know are down
And I say to them, get a hold of yourself,
For no one is listening.

Don 't be
Down,
Or you will be down
All by yourself.

That's the nature of today's community
In America
The music,
Has died, at least in most places.

Gone are the days,
Even in Dublin,

When James Joyce could pack it all into
24 hours, and call it Ulysses….

I went to a movie on a date
On the West Side
In 1975, holding hands
Holding hands, holding hands.

I woke up
In 2017
With nothing
In my hands.

The same hands
That wrote all the books that sit above my head
With a light on them
They look nice.

In my little place
Just
Them
And me.

She was my world
In 1975
And then I went
To see other worlds.

And wrote about them
See
Just above my head
And I forget what she looks like.

But remember she said
Its
"just you
And me, Ted"

Kiss me
And lets live
Forever
And ever.

The music will never stop
Sip the red wine
Smile and kiss
Smile and kiss.

The blue jays have just returned
There, in the palm trees
Just them
And me.

And the letters on the page
Rolling off the fingers
Just to say
Fill the page.

And every week someone dies
As if a bomb was dropped
And all my friends
Disappeared.

But that is life
Get over it
A little voice
Says.

And everyone is preparing for war
As if
It's
1913.

I can't believe I was once
Loved by you
Oh beautiful Lady
so far above this animal called me.

So lucky you are
Not to be
With
Me.

Hard to believe you used to say
Being with me was like
Life, for the first time
Now all I have, are the birds.

Who come to me
And try to speak
Of life
Beyond death.

Enough... this very next morning
In the middle of February, sitting
In outside little garden
When

And this poem was begun
On February 20, 1916
And on this very day
February 20, 1917

Up a tree always barren of any birds
Sat three
Two fat Blue jays
And one lovely fat lady with an orange body and gray feathers.

It happened, like a
Revelation,
It was real
Not fiction, I saw.

But the world is like
It was,
In 1912 ??
1913??

Somewhere in the time
Before,
It all unraveled,
In 1914.

And the entire
20 century

Failed it's civilization
And humanity went crazy.

Is 2017??
On the cusp?
Intellectuals don't think past
Their next paper,
And politicians are into self AN GRAND DIZ MENT.

And we are all here
Looking in
As they control
Television, television, television.

The professors are hiding behind
Their power-point presentations
The students don't mind
For they are playing games on their devices.

But, its here again
Just like 1912
Or close in
To 1914.

It was just a memory
Of a history
Taught, a long time ago,
And its coming back, coming back.

Millions upon millions of displaced roaming families
From ravages of war
Like now
As bodies of sweet souls wash up upon vacation beaches.

Not just Blue jays confused
 Woodcocks flying north
Too soon
Dying in freezing snow and ice.

It was January 1962
I was given a book on Modern European History

To teach, as a professor of history
To wide-eyed innocent men,

With a three-piece vested suit
White collar and silk tie
English leather shoes
For the show at hand,

A new one, for a twenty-six year
old military veteran,
Two weeks out of college
With the most important job in the world.

Blood, sweat, and tears,
Words shot into eager but surprised eyes
to open to, how young men their age
killed each other by the millions, millions, millions.

Interesting, the business majors all said
And so relieved
That, this
Would never happen, again.

55 years later
Business majors no longer have to hear
For its just a "Flat World" now
Without the passions of the flesh.

Ignorance may be bliss
Just like a kiss
But, this can be, like the kiss
Of death.

My neighbor then, from sixty two to 1964
Old John McNichol, had been an ambulance
Driver in WW I, and often took me to an old cottage
On the estate

Where his WW I comrade lived
All alone,
With his missing leg,
And gas damaged lungs, waiting, with a bottle of whiskey.

I listened to the old man
And tried to infuse Carlton J. Hayes' history
Book from which I taught,
With deeper lessons than any academic could learn.

The Blue jays have returned
And the times have returned
And it will not be only the refugees and
Woodcocks, but just like

Wars of old
And streams of helpless souls
In old trucks in deep depression days of the thirties
Walking, walking, eyes, empty, and confused.

How could it be?
How could it happen?
What happened?
How could this happen to me, and my family?

Hopelessly, I tried to get students to try and feel
The hopeless pain suffered by tens of millions
Of parents
Who lost their sons.

None could understand how that felt
Nor, I, whose only son was just born
Never then
Knowing what lie ahead, in my own ignorance.

Of loosing
An only son,
Like Mary and Joseph and
Job, and others in deep literature and the bible.

Last week we dropped the largest non-nuc bomb
Ever dropped anytime, anyplace,
Is that not just great?
"Make America Great Again"

Last week our government gave sleaze-bag debt collectors
The business of collecting any money owed to the IRS
so if you owe a dollar, close your windows, shut off your phone,
hide your auto, take your money out of the bank.

They will hunt you down
Like we did Saddam
Qadhafi
And "The Fugitive," may God rest their souls, and yours.

Roses are red
Violets are blue
Like poetry used to be
Like the times we watched the Blue jays return.

When the whole world was going to be "democratic"
Or else
We would see that they do
As the bombs blew.

On babies, on mommies, on
The old
To give them
The right to vote.

What about the rights
To a toilet
To a roof over one's family
A place to cook and a place to sleep?

Oh?
The decision-makers forget that?
Freedoms of speech, press, and assembly
Was all people wanted.

But who wants to talk, write, and assemble
With no toilet
No roof
No place to cook and sleep.

Used to go to friend's homes

And they would want to show you
Photos from their vacation
Now, they want to show you their guns.

As a 70's song went, "I'm just a writer
Trapped within my youth."
With all the pains life
Brings forth.

And still the hope
A little boy feels
When the sun shines on his eyes
At the water's edge.

So arrogant us humans
To not recognize our oneness with all
Of nature,
Even the leaves on the trees.

Many believe their dogs and cats understand them
But what about the plants
And the trees,
They see us, they hear us, perhaps read our simple minds.

Outside, a small lizard climbs onto a leaf of a plant
As green as the plant, not "as" but green, green
Itself, as part of the plant
Knowing something, as we should.

And beneath the lizard's throat drops
A red and white piece of skin
Why? Only nature knows, but perhaps a warning
To us, the red, danger, we seem close to 1914.

But this time,
Not just entire towns young male population
Never returns from the battlefields
Of Europe.

We all done,
For the humans now have the nucs

They did not have in 1914
Does the lizard sense this????

They say white men can't jump
And they don't get that lump
In their throat
For those who love them.

Did you ever see a white athlete
After the game won,
Thank his Mom or Grandma?
Any???

There was Tak McKinley, UCLA
In the pro football draft, this big dude
Who tears up men of the field
With a huge photo

Of his grandma,
Who raised him after being abandoned
Her huge photo he carried during the ceremonies
Think: what a man. What love.

Come on my white brothers
Tell me,
Not just us with Irish moms
But all of you.

Just came back from St. Croix, Virgin Islands
And after years in brutal south Florida
I met brothers and sister I want to live among,
Such love I received. Such openness.

What's happening America
We don't reach out
We are suspicious
We are closed up.

The blue jays are beginning to leave for
Up north
Where Trump and the Republicans have no idea
About the realities of geopolitics.

And in Europe
The ancient forces of tribal and ethnic forces
Are encouraging the Russians and Turks
To retake the territories of their empires.

And what has this to do with birds?
With flowers and trees and sunsets
Love and life
The essence of poetry?

Perhaps just ask the migrants
Living behind razor wire fences in Hungary
Whose empty eyes and fear I once saw in 1956
After the Russians destroyed their revolution.

Less the Hungarians forget
They once were migrants
And came in multitudes to the U.S.
I saw, I remember; but do they?

Roses are red
Violets are blue
As the professors teach
In poetry 101.

Or as the old Cherokee taught his grandson
"my grandson, there is a battle between two
Wolves inside us all, one is evil. It is anger, jealousy,
Greed, resentment, inferiority, lies, and ego."

"The other wolf is good, it is joy, peace, love
Humility, empathy, and truth. The boy thought
Then asked, 'Grandfather, which wolf wins?'
The old man quietly replied, the one you feed."

Or as another teacher informed
For all writers to
Awaken
To their inner selves

"To survive, you must

Tell stories."
Umberto Eco
Taught me: "must tell stories," to survive.

To survive ... wow
Not just the present
But the past and the unknown
Future.

Or, the illusion
That it can be separated
For it is one,
Say not just Albert, but the Maori.

Yesterday, I was visited by one pretty
Blue jay, alone on a branch in a small
Bush, reminding me, that one is ok,
And less, ok too.

And today she came back
Just like nature
Itself, unless humans
Destroy their habitats.

like I once viewed
off a ship
in McMurdo
Bay, back then.

When New Zealand
Declared a nuclear free zone
And we were trying to
Save the world.

Before everyone had
Their eyes and noses
And minds, into
Their smart phones.

Barnum & Bailey Circus came to an end
So sad
After 146

Years.

I remember my favorite uncle, my father's
Older brother, George, taking me
To the circus,
When I was six.

Never had much fun in those days
Of discipline, beatings, nasty nuns
Bullies,
And total unhappiness.

Except, that day with uncle George,
Fun and laughs, and he taught me
To order drinks without ice,
To get one's money's worth.

Old George drank himself to
Death in Camden,
Where Walt Whitman is buried
Another happy guy.

"Only the lonely, know why I cry"
Sang Roy Orbison a long time ago,
But maybe today
More lonely people than ever?

The young adults are living with
Their parents, no talk of "going out
To the coast" like the old days,
Instead, they do drugs and sit in one place.

And worry about paying their loans
But back then, we just said
Fxxx it,
And lived for the day, and laughed a lot.

Today, the only ones who smile a lot
Are the guys on the business pages
Always smiling, yeah,
For they are happy to be screwing us all.

Does anyone major in history? Anthropology?
English? Anymore?
Their the ones the bill collectors go after
How dare them dream of better worlds.

Now with Jeff Sessions in power
Maybe we could have some debtor prisons
To puts those god dam humanity majors
In jail till they pay their college loans.

Funny? Hell no,
This is the new America
Rounding up five year old children and their
Latino mothers and sending them

Back to where they belong, in San Pedro Sula
Honduras, so say the politicians who
Have never seen San Pedro Sula,
Or set foot there, to get shot at, or cut.

Cut? Ho ho... a gal pulled a knife
And cut me
On a date,
After we came from dinner.

And my pal, the chief of police,
Named Rodriquez, who was holding my books
For me after I escaped with my life,
Was shot and killed last year.

Or so many people around me when I lived
In Honduras, who were shot, stabbed, and killed,
So close, always so close,
And that's where these political bastards

Want to send the Latino mother
And her five year old daughter
Back, to where
They belong... Jeff Sessions... Jeff Sessions,

And lets not forget Donald Trump
Who started all this

I predicted his win, for I am a prophet
Who regrets his prediction.

Roses are red,
Violets are blue
And the Blue jays are coming and
Going.

And you New York critics
Can kiss my
Irish ass
For I, call this, poetry.

It started in Dublin
With a Guinness in my hand
And my Irish passport next to my heart
Before I knew I had to flee back home.

And then on to the mountains of Western
Carolina, until near DUI's and stupid lady named
Blondi who sang dumb redneck songs, and then to
St. Croix, and near death collision, and back

To Hollywood Florida
And silence
Pushing my body in the hot sun as if I were
A boy, with a rebirth everyday swimming in the sea.

No rebirth in Manchester,
Oh sweet family loved young souls taken from us
By a Muslim Libyan sub-human,
Bastard, bastard, bastard, your soul to a pit in hell.

Be your family shamed forever,
Young lovely little girls, budding teenagers,
Sparkles of love in our world, taken from the
Arms of their loved ones,

Bastard, bastard, bastard, your soul to pit in hell.
And there we will find you
And watch you suffer for hurting such
Innocent, innocent, innocent, beautiful humans.

Speaking of beautiful human beings,
Today we honor them, "Memorial Day,"
All our guys and gals who gave their lives
For America. For you. For me, For all of us.

So we could use our lives as we wished,
Swish, swish ….ed…ed time goes
By so fast
What did we wish?

Yes beauty, no pain,
But life is not fair, nor predictable,
And the best of it, and the worst of it,
Are turned into art.

And what does art do??????
"It expands the scope of life
And distills its beauty & it's pain,"
The philosopher, A.O. Scott reveals to us.

"distills," reduces it so we can touch it,
Hold it, slow down this life force, which only
Art can do….like making love
In the afternoon.

I saw her face walk by the window
Once pretty when young, now confused
Walking behind old parents
Who still pay the mortgage.

As least she is alive here in old Hollywood
Where the laughing voices and fun
Loving folks have, well, just
Disappeared.

They didn't exercise in the hot sun to sweat
The poisons from their bodies or plunge their
Bodies into the expensive pools they maintained
Or just jump in the sea so near, and so healthy.

53

They ate and drank, ate and drank,
And slept a lot, they did
And smoked those filtered cigs,
But I loved them,

A lot,
And thought they would live
Forever,
But now their spaces are empty, and lonely.

Yesterday I saw several curvy scantily clad
Young beautiful girls on a hot beach
Soon thereafter, joined by several handsome
Young smiling guys, And then,

My mind tricked me into seeing a similar scene
But it was many years ago, when we were all
Young, he a muscular Irish U.S. Marine and she a
Dark haired white skinned New Orleans's "Lady."

I fixed em up, back then, her so lady, he so animal,
And the last time I saw them together, she
Insisted I look at him…"He loved you," she
Said, say goodbye to him….in his burial box.

But it was just yesterday with a salty wind
Blowing off the tips of Ocean City waves, her
Long dark hair flowing to her young legs
 Their passion hidden by smiles and laughter.

As I saw yesterday,
Yes,
Just,
Yesterday, whatever that means anymore.

And nowadays when I see a very special young
Female rear end on the beach, I just accept
That god made them like that, so young men

Lust, so the human race grows.

For even
Blue jays, chase
Each other
Around.

Sometimes too many
And loose the
One,
They really want.

Or
As us humans
Say
The one we love.

I have seen so much human suffering
And longing for one's loving others
Whose lives were dimmed or lost
Leaving grieving lost souls loving in a void.

Confused
Alone
And in complete
Bewilderment,

At this condition
We
Call
Being human.

Radical Islam knows nothing about
Being human
They preach of a God who
Who like them, hates, hates, hates.

They kill nice people on the streets
Of London, Paris, Manchester,
Orlando, San Bernardino,

Why? They have deep shame.

Shame, what Officer Jeronimo Yanez

Should feel... pulled over Philando Castile
For a broken taillight, "broken taillight,"
Yanez fired multiple bullets into his body.

Philando and his girlfriend where just
Stoned from good herb, peaceful, silly
Perhaps, and then officer Yanez pumped
Nine bullets into Philando's body

And at the trial
Yanez walked
From his
Murder, of this man.

Violence all over the place
A long long road from
Peace and love
Peace and love, oh flower children.

I rarely see lovers holding hands,
Or strangers smiling
Just smiling,
But a lot of anger in cars.

But there are nice young Afro-American
Girls at MacDonald's
Being just themselves
And nice to nasty customers.

In America's culture
When people get old
They may well be viewed
As another species.

By the young
Who believe they
Will never
Get there.

Who should be out there protesting

Five generations of young American's dying
In Afghanistan, for what?
And how much longer?

Now over sixteen years,
Will it go to twenty years?
Thirty years? Did only the novelist James Mitchener know
That no one changes Afghanistan.

Especially now, with Trump hiding
From his responsibility as
Commander In Chief, abrogating
His duty to the military.

Military know how to fight
But war is more about politics
Man can't think of politics when
In the midst of a street fight.

Diplomats, are a rare breed of humans
Who study what others believe and will
Fight for, and find avenues to listen
And attempt to understand, the passions.

So hatred can be addressed
With respect, so all who hate
Can somehow,
Find an inch or agreement, preventing death.

That's why our Constitution
Created a
Commander In chief
Oh hell, were are the Blue jays?

For the guy we elected in 2016
Is the very opposite of
John F. Kennedy, who saved us from
Nuclear annihilation in 1962.

What will happen in the next four years

Only the spirits know
And perhaps you should just
Pour yourself a drink.

The madness, in Afghanistan alone,
Taliban stronger and sicker than ever
Attacking hospitals killing doctors
And patients alike.

Where are the blue jays
Where the doves of peace
Where is
Sanity, in 2017.

In Jerusalem,
 Three men walk out of Aqsa Mosque
And kill two police guarding
This sacred place.

Temple Mount to the Jews
The Noble Sanctuary to Muslims
Men with weapons
Emerging from a place of worship???The old man said "life is short."
Yes, we hear, but who believes
Until
Your' looking at the end.

Is 2017 anything
Like
1913?
1914?

Do Blue jays matter?
Does nature matter?
What's wrong with
Human nature?

Young men study history
And then, go on to repeat it
Over and over and over
Again.

How long since I began this poem
Now, August 6th, year later
(theme?? A blue jay appeared
Just when I have given up.. screaming..

Boys grow up, but their ego's often never do
And become leaders of countries
And forget the lessons from the books
And take the young men to war, again.

Maybe it is time
For all women to rule
Like the tribal leaders of my Maori brothers
Who learned from the carnage of WW I.

When all the men from the Ngai Tuhoe tribe who
Went off to ww I
Never
Came home again.

So, in WW II
Princess Tapula said
No
You can't take my boys again.

And in 2017, American boys are dying
In a country that stones women to death
Mutilates young female gentiles, and covers
Women's heads and bodies so they are ghosts.

American troops are dying at the hands
Of Afghanistan men and boys who are not
Foreign invaders, but Afghan men and boys
Who destroy schools and kill education

But, like Woodrow Wilson in WW I,
We are making the world "safe for Democracy"
Hey, a girl cannot show her face
enough for Democracy, or duck the acid thrown.

Meanwhile, powerful armies are gathering

All around the globe, like men in heat
Missiles are fired into space, nuclear
Weapons are being modernized.

And here I am in Hollywood Florida
Working-out in the mid-day sun
Trying to sweat out the poisons
Of age, just to write again, tomorrow.

And moving to the source *true*
Of my first novel
To smell the air and hear the birds
In a few days, I will be home again.

After a year of searching,
First to Dublin Ireland,
Then the mountains of Western Carolina
Finally, St Croix, Virgin Islands.

As my beloved pals of a lifetime
Have died
Leaving me
Alone, without their wisdom and love.

Leaving another, mean, hate filled, vicious
Florida property owner
This one a "witch" called Rosemary
From Portugal, filled with hate.

A novel about hurricane "Sandy,"
Now facing "Irma"
Is life unpredictable
Or not?

Left Hollywood Lakes area
34 years ago
Brutal foreclosure chapter
In "Semineaux Miami"

And oh, how I resist telling
The truth, about my wishing
A giant hurricane came and
Destroyed the Lakes.

Now, that I moved back
But a week ago,
Hurricane Irma is threatening
To do just that.

What's the
Moral here?
What's the lesson?
Only a few days will tell.

Get back to Irma…wow…. I used
To write about Chinese and American
Foreign policy, then "Escaping Hurricane
Sandy," … what to do with Irma?

She killed
Not just souls
But dreams
That will never unfold

Crushed not just things
Man-made and nature itself
Leaving us lying to ourselves
That we survived her

Even those
Who fear not death
Now
Fear this shadow that hangs

In the hidden recesses of
Our minds
Like a large silent
Black leopard

Taking away all the mysteries
And exposing life
As not just a single bite
Of a shit sandwich, one day

But ongoing

From wind and water in Puerto Rico
Earthquakes
In Mexico.

And the sweetest Islanders I
Have ever met, in the
Atlantic or Pacific oceans,
My brothers and sisters of St. Croix.

As President Trump
Threatens to wipe
North Korea, off the
Map, as if he is God.

Then, sitting in my truck
With this despairing feeling
A beautiful Blue Jay gently landed on
A branch, and spoke to me of peace.

The following day, a small flock of noisy
Green patriots swopped down to the
Field, as they had done in Key Largo
Some time ago.

Trying to hold onto the moments
Of tranquility as a gift of
Nature
In a world moving so fast

And worse, everything
In a disintegration mode
Coming apart
Or in outright confrontation.

What to make of the fact
That NY city schools report
A big increase in number
Of weapons carried in by students.

Even old NY state Village of Whitesboro
Changed the old sea of a white man
Besting an Indian in a wrestling match

To one with more equal image.

Even in the hills of peaceful wine
Country in Oregon
Friction with newcomer wanting
To harvest the sacred herb.

Is it all one?
Hurricanes, earthquakes,
A divided Washington that fails
And drives us further apart.

Where do we turn?
When the leader of the free world
Stakes his claim on fighting everyone
Including athletes who give us relief

Where? Oh God
Are the peacemakers?
Maybe its time for women
To rule, except old Hillary.

I became a man as a fighter
In the streets and in the ring
Where men respect each other
And develop true love for each other.

And know I see weak men, very
Insecure men, men with distorted egos
Proud faces of men who could not
Hold their own in a dark alley

Threatening... standing against
The weak and helpless
Talking tough, to people, children
Who just need a hug

But who, I ask, will bring us
Together? Please help me.

Bring peace; and to think I used
To work on Peacekeeping for the

Director of Political and Security Affairs
At the United Nations.

But do not know how to bring
Peace to our communities
In America
In this century starting off so violently.

Even love. Men don't feel love from
Women. Women get love from other
Women. But hey, who are making
The babies? Life goes on.

I once had a professor of English
Who dressed the part and looked the part
Who talked of meaning in words
As if we had only minds, and no bodies.

I recently was to move to St Croix
Or perhaps Puerto Rico
By Irma and Maria made me grateful
That neither occurred.

But, oh my soul does weep
For so many sweet people
Who need our help, more
Than just our weeps.

Socrates, Aristotle, and Plato
Did not pontificate on a mountaintop
But spoke during horrible strife,
Suffering, wars….to find answers.

As we must now,
With Trump promoting hatred
And Latino's being captured and
Interned for exile

Not to concentration camps like
The Nazis': but hey
Is all life not just
Relative??

Where in the universe would I be
If old Joe Gladue and old Philip
McDermott had faced the border
Controls that hatred has created??

Speaking of hatred, Afghanistan is
Always a default setting, as Muslim killers
Disguised as shepherds attending to their flock
Attacked a Shite mosque in Kabul

As worshipers were leaving
Their prayer session, a shepherd set off a bomb
Killing many innocent people just trying to pray
To their God, the bastard was also killed.

It's October now in South Florida and many
Of the pretty anxious birds are returning,
my Blue jays
and Green Parrots.

But yesterday I slowly drove past
A woman in a car by the water
I slowed for a moment
For she was so sad.

Her hand beneath her nose
Head slightly shaking from
The turmoil of some unbearable
Pain, tears I could not see.

A thirty something pudgy Latin
Woman, in such desperate despair
Hurt, hurt, hurt, I could not only
See, but feel.

What did I do?
Drove off
And said a prayer
For her.

What a coward, I am, so
Guilty I feel today, what the hell am
I ? Anyway. Why did I no back up
And walk over

And tell her, " Hi, I am sorry you
Are hurt. But you are not alone
God bless you. Please know that
Mary and the angels are looking,

After you" ...
You get through this moment,
These hours, .. ok?   You will
Be ok Miss,

Know, you are not alone
God bless you and good bye"
And Oh God, give me the grace and
Wisdom and courage, to do that in the future.

Rather than be the coward
I was yesterday
Along the Inland waterway canal
In Dania Florida.

Its nearing the end of October,
Again, in South Florida,
And many birds are returning
Slowly

Even nature confused
No cold waves triggered their
Migratory instincts, flying
From summer to summer.

On the west coast
Fleeing fire
Huge and deadly
Birds and humans alike.

On the Atlantic side,
They drown
Just like

Us.

"Great disorder under the Heavens"
The ancient Chinese philosophers viewed
As portents for the future
Danger lies ahead.

To them, collapse of the Empire
To us
A nuclear war
Or WW III.

It ain't the prediction of an ideologue
Or some dumb bastard on TV, but
One who has studied the world for
More years than wishes to disclose.

Scary times,
Hidden in the womb of
Civilizations long gone, warnings
Too subtle for the noise of the airways

Some say so what to me, I've lived
A full life
But hell, how about my children,
Grandchildren, and great grandchildren?

Or my young bride
With whom I may have
More
Children.

The problem is that most look into the
Deep cavern of death,
And a few of us look to the heavens
With hope and love.

If the world becomes a scorched earth

Of fires and floods
Death and destruction
A few of us will survive, with love and compassion.

In our hearts
In our minds
In our resolve
To keep life on earth, alive.

The Blue jays have followed
Forget this talk of war
We moved north to
Panama City.

From the hell of south Florida
To the heaven in the
Panhandle...
Where people smile, peace here.

From a war zone
To land of peace
From the Harding street witch
And the South Lake witch

To a house in the country
Someone pinch me
Is this for real
Or make-believe.

Up in the panhandle
Where everything and everyone
Is real
Though sometimes boring.

But then look at the world
Most cannot, in fact how many
Actually read about the suffering, wars,
Killings, children, children, Americans

We ignore the horror of their seeing
Their children suffering, dying, dying
In their arms, my fellow Americans

We will suffer the same horrible pain.

Bullshit, you may think
Far away
But, like a virus far far away
Is comes, with all the pain and sorry we ignored.

But the truth may be
That all these wars in 2018
Are just the beginning
So enjoy

Your electricity, your clean water, your
Stores stocked with food
Our nights free of violence as we sleep
In a peace, than may not be forever.

Speaking of real, watched Elton John
On Steven Colbert's late night show
and there is this amazing singer
we all love

just like everything else today
blurred beneath all the flashing
lights, musicians playing, too noisy
tinny, everything flashing

flashing, obscuring the wonderful
voice, now weaker with age
Elton, a performance like everything
else, in this age of Trump, hollow.

I see the Blue jays here in Panama City
They came to my bamboo trees
And flashed
A look at me

saw my heart hardened like steel
As a man of the world watching it all
Crumbling

Like it did in 1914, yes it's a repeat.

And I don't wish to repeat that theme
Again: but it's hard for the Blue jays or
Any of nature's healing beauty
In sight, sound, or silence

To bring me the peace I crave
Reading in-depth news reporting from
Around the world each morning,
Studying it for knowledge and understanding

Used to be: to get my mind off
Personal pain or worries
See so much out there, out there
And here in our worlds

Before allowing my mind to
Rest, so I can work and write
And dream
Of better things.

I always like to see
In rainbows, and silly
Songs I like to sing
Each day.

But now I see our world
More pain than in I have
Ever seen, except in history
Books long ago dumbed as trash

Panama City today, on back of two vehicles
"reject hate, let's come together in peace"
Image of gun pointing at you; "nothing in this truck worth dying for"
Then a sign for a church: "The Real God."

A week later confrontation with mortality
Behind that wall, hordes of depression, as has happened
Before in my life, bringing fear and worry, until, a red Cardinal
Flew next to me, again, it happened.

Must be my son
Coming, when I am on the edge of

Life, looking into
Eternity, and always a red Cardinal

Remember sitting behind a bamboo screen in the rear
Of my Gloucester City home on the river,
Peeking between small openings, snow on rocks
Tears rolling down, and then, big red Cardinal.

Brings me back to the reality that I must live
Must fight depression
Must fight death wishes
Must look up at the blue sky.

The Blue jays are returning
But the rare and beautiful red Cardinals
Bring this poem to an end
Of pain, and new resolve to live

And love
All around me
Like my Ta Moko I wear around my neck
From my Maori tribe in New Zealand.

We are never alone,
Surrounded by family, friends, kind strangers
The mountains, the trees, sky, clouds
Stars, moons, the universe, and ki' Wa.

John (lets bomb the world) Bolton wants to
Bomb North Korea, but "Red Velvet" dancers and singers
Are shaking their botties and rear cheeks to bring
Some peace to the peninsula.

Bolton: shows that the weakest of men
Are the most dangerous
Especially those who never fought
Bolton, a man who would bolt in the face of the enemy.

Like that other coward
A while back
Called Dick Chaney
Two men not worth a penny.

And then we fast-forward to Hurricane Michael
My living in Panama City, destroyed
Beyond imagination, now sitting in a
Park in Coral Springs.

Six hundred miles south
In denial, of what had just happened under the
Violence called Hurricane Michael
After the other two,

For "Sandy" was nasty,
"Irma was dangerous"
And "Michael," was
A killer,

I sat through,
And survived,
But not without my denial
Oh, not that again.

That which the VA shrinks finally recognized
After two years of analysis
PTSD from military combat
Just shortly before "Michael,"

Whose power was unmatched of any before
Looked like Hiroshima without the corpuses
Violating even the codes of mother nature
With trees as thick as trucks snapping like twigs

And deep in my mind
Something snapped, from this bastard storm

What group sang,
" Life goes on
Long after the fun of living
Is gone."

Even in old Key West I saw last week
Where once sailors fishermen adventurers punched
Each other in street fights over women or card cheating
Now, the successful ones are here

But waited too long
Long sad or confused faces, old, looking
Eyes fixated on nothingness, turning once wild streets
Of Key West into a place of rest, and boredom it become.

Like most other places today,
Except perhaps, County Monaghan
Or perhaps
County Roscommon, then see me smile.

Looking for Blue jays
Come singing my way
Today
Or, any day.

The end?
Or just the beginning?

ETG

ACKNOWLEDGEMENTS

" A James Joyce 24 hour inspiration," yes; this is the core of my acknowledgements, the author of such works as "The Dubliners" and "Ulysses," that inspired this book of poetry while I was in Dublin, not as a tourist but as an Irish citizen intending to settle and work there indefinitely, having flown in on a one-way ticket from Fr Lauderdale/Hollywood, with my new Irish passport having just been issued in April 2014.

One of the proudest moments of my life, when the Irish Customs Officer looked at my passport, then said: "Welcome Home," with a big Irish grin on his face, me smiling like a kid in a candy shop, till my thoughts of both my grandparents, Mary Kelly of County Monaghan and Philip McDermott of County Roscommon came front and center into my third eye; they, in 1888, not far from this airport, walking onto a ship embarking for America, he with his four brothers, her with her sisters, not knowing each other at the time, each with pain in their hearts and tensions in their bodies as they descended into the dark, inhospitable, narrow, damp, threatening bowls of the ship called steerage; their young minds, lungs, and bodies used to being outdoors on the farmlands of Ireland, surrounded by family and neighbors, with their only enemies , famine, starvation, and the British who caused it.

My motivations for relocating to Dublin were stacked one upon the other. Since childhood I could never be satisfied with being in one place but had to explore beyond the neighborhood, over the fences, across the tracks, joining the military at 18 not out of patriotism but a wish to see the world, followed by working as a diver looking for gold and silver in Caribbean waters from long sunken Spanish galleons, later sailing the seven seas as a Merchant Marine, then traveling the world for the UN, then after publication of a book on nuclear politics being invited to New Zealand and the Pacific to help prevent a nuclear war, then during the Cold War traveling the world teaching US Naval and Airforce officers; pilots, submariners, nuclear missile operators about Russians and Chinese, and it goes on and on.

Dublin? Perhaps, I will learn something about this compulsion to travel, for there is much Viking blood in the Irish, Scandinavian peoples from what is now Norway, who attacked undefended wealthy monasteries in Dublin; the Norse attacking the east and south coasts while the Danes drove further inland with their shallow-drafted Longboats, eventually establishing a settlement at Longport that offered easy access to the open sea.

In fact, the Longport settlement marks the foundation date of the city of Dublin. The towns of Cork, Limerick, Wexford and Waterford were all set up before 900, all with a Viking foundation, and even though the native Irish drove the Viking out of Longport in 902, the Vikings remained part of the Irish experience for three centuries, and turned the Irish Sea into a Viking lake, with the new town of Dublin a center of commerce. So perhaps, my restlessness stems in part from my Irish blood, itself infused with Viking restlessness? In time, my living in Dublin may reveal something.

On more mundane levels, I had a friend of a friend who was in the process of setting up a few Irish pubs where I would be welcomed to poet my poetry and sell my books of poetry, novels and politics, and I had a scheduled interview at Trinity College to possibly teach courses on international politics and China, and I had a book of poems in my head to be set in Dublin.

And then there was the German/Spanish connection. When teaching on the military bases in Europe I had begun a Cold War spy novel that I had put aside to write my novels set in Miami and New Zealand, intending it to be volume three of my trilogy before taking my character back in time to 261 BC China with the "Birth of China," so with being an Irish citizen with a base in Dublin, I could eventually drive to Germany and Spain to retrace spy novel long ago discarded.

So I had a lot of reasons to settle in Dublin. But, I have always had a built in sense that tells me very quickly if I should remain in a country or leave. Landing in New Zealand to deliver two talks, I stayed a year. Landing in Central America, I stayed three years. Landing in Heidelberg Germany for a day, I stayed a year. Landing in Dublin with all the above reasons to stay, I left in 24 hours.

In those 24 hours I learned much; and as one old Irishman told me in a pub over mugs of Guinness, after talking with me for an hour: " You learned more about Dublin in 24 hours than many who have lived here for 24 years." And then he told me, that became the basis for this very poetry book, " I have someone for you to meet, just show up outside your hotel in an hour and I will take you to see him.

That "him," turned out to be Dublin's greatest interpreter of James Joyce's famous novel, "Ulysses." And what a character he is: the performance artist, Robert Gogan, who brought to life for me not only the silly-ass characters in Joyce's "Ulysses," but the down home sexual desires of Molly Bloom as she ends her day in a dreamy reality all her own, and Gogan brought tears to my eyes describing the crazy and funny aspects of Joyce's novel that are the backbone of the novel; Joyce himself once stating that, "There is not one serious line in it."

Over more than a few Irish whiskeys spanning an hour Gogan appeared somewhat taken back by the fact that I had been in Dublin short of 24 hours, and that somehow, strangely, I felt new poems wanting to emerge out of my heart, soul, mind; especially my subconscious, but: I was going to leave. This is when Gogan told me a well-known fact that most know, but I did not: that "Ulysses" all took place in Dublin in just 24 hours. I was startled when he informed me of this basic fact I had never known.

" Mate, " Gogan said with a huge smile on his Irish mug, " when you leave here, you will be carrying a million, of what I call, James Joyce 'seeds of discovery,' that many would like to have, but only a few experience, those whom Joyce himself has infected with his madness. It will not be till you go back to America that these seeds will pop out of you. No one will believe you, but that is what has happened to you."

"Thank you Robert," I had no intention of writing about this strange Dublin experience, but: here it is, for better or for worse, a James Joyce inspiration that would have made the philosopher Jung quite pleased.

Memorial Day, May 27, 2019

RELATED POEMS FROM "Poetry in Green: Poetry & Stories from around the world."

NOW THAT I AM AN IRISHMAN

(The day I became a citizen of Ireland)
June , 2013

Not just on St Patrick's Day, but everyday
Today, tomorrow, and forever

For today I became an Irish citizen,
125 years after my grandparents landed on Ellis Island

From a brutal sail in the bottom of a rat infested
Ship, then came, same ship, never met on the sail, never.

Phillip McDermott and Mary Kelly, County Roscommon
And County Monahan, escaping starvation and English rule
So today, I celebrate for them, with the writing of this poem
And a few empty glasses tonight.

I could not celebrate becoming an American
For new-born babies are not allowed to drink in America

And I was not yet verbal then, but now that I am an Irishman
I can speak with authority, fast, and with an uncanny wisdom.

And now that I am an Irishman I can laugh at folly
And smile upon tragedy.

Now that I am an Irishman
I can tell the British to stick it where they sit

Now that I am an Irishman
I can dance with the young lassies and down a few pints of Guiness

Now that I am an Irishman
I can be proud of my political savy and brilliant mind

Now that I am an Irishman
I can stick my finger in the eyes of common sense

Now that I am an Irishman
I can tell the Pope to kiss my Irish ...for all the child molesters

Now that I am an Irishman\
I no longer have to punch the red head for calling me a Dago

Now that I am an Irishman
I bough my head in respect to the Irish spirits of creativity

Now that I am an Irishman
I pray to Joyce, Yeats, Heany, to keep me believing.

Now that I am an Irishman

I feel no guilt for having a drink with all above & those beneath.

Now that I am an Irishman
I must say, Mate; I am an Irish poet; for better or for worse.

Now that I am an Irishman
I know how tough it is to get a kiss from a fine lady

Now that I am an Irishman

The inspiration for this poem was the thought of my Grandparents generation who came to America and never again saw their parents or family. They got jobs, raised families, often very large families and never returned to the "old country" as I remember my mother and her sisters saying. I wish they were alive now so I could be precise in my questions but all I have is this very vague memory of a few whispering conversations that never seemed to get down to the core, for it would involve too much self-indulgence or some other shadows of the Irish soul, best kept unspoken. Realistically of course, in their day before intercontinental flights, it would have had to be a trip by sea; and here their memories were often of brutal voyages that seemed to never end, or perhaps the money.

IRISH HARPS

Today, I applied for my Irish passport
to sail to an Irish port.

I am sitting by a wharf
on a sea wall, feeling so like a dwarf

So small and so far north
near a star my ancestors held forth

To follow the sun to the west
where all the sons, and all the daughters

Went…went…and never came back
never came back…never came back.

America, America what have you
done with our sons?

America, America what have you
done with out daughters?

They have sailed north, they sailed
west…now they are at rest.

Never coming home, never coming home,
our sons and our daughters.

But look out upon the waters
their grandchildren speak

Seek to know ye, old
Ireland, our genes seek, seek.

To know ye mate, to
know ye lass, be you a Kelly or a McDermott

We are sailing south, we are flying
east, to bring some peace.

To the adventurous spirits that
came our way like needles in the hay.

And grew to win the day in
politics, in power, and …made it, their way.

To send us back this way
just to show you, we are you,

With our passports next to our hearts
that pump a blood, filled

With Irish Harps

ETG , 4/11/2014, Atlantic City, E. Ted Gladue

Made in the USA
Middletown, DE
16 June 2019